Musical Kaleidoscope

COLORING BOOK

Jeremy Elder

Dover Publications, Inc.
Mineola, New York

Strings. Brass. Percussion. Woodwinds. Flip through the thirty-one illustrations in this coloring book and you'll see them all burst from the page in symphonic symmetry. With so many opportunities to experiment, why not try traditional colors for one instrument and then add a custom "paint-job" to another? And for a quick quiz, see if you can name each instrument before checking the answer provided near the page perforations. Once you're finished, simply tear out the page and display your work.

Bibliographical Note

Musical Kaleidoscope Coloring Book is a new work, first published by Dover Publications, Inc., in 2018.

International Standard Book Number

ISBN-13: 978-0-486-81889-4
ISBN-10: 0-486-81889-6

Manufactured in the United States by LSC Communications
81889602   2018
www.doverpublications.com

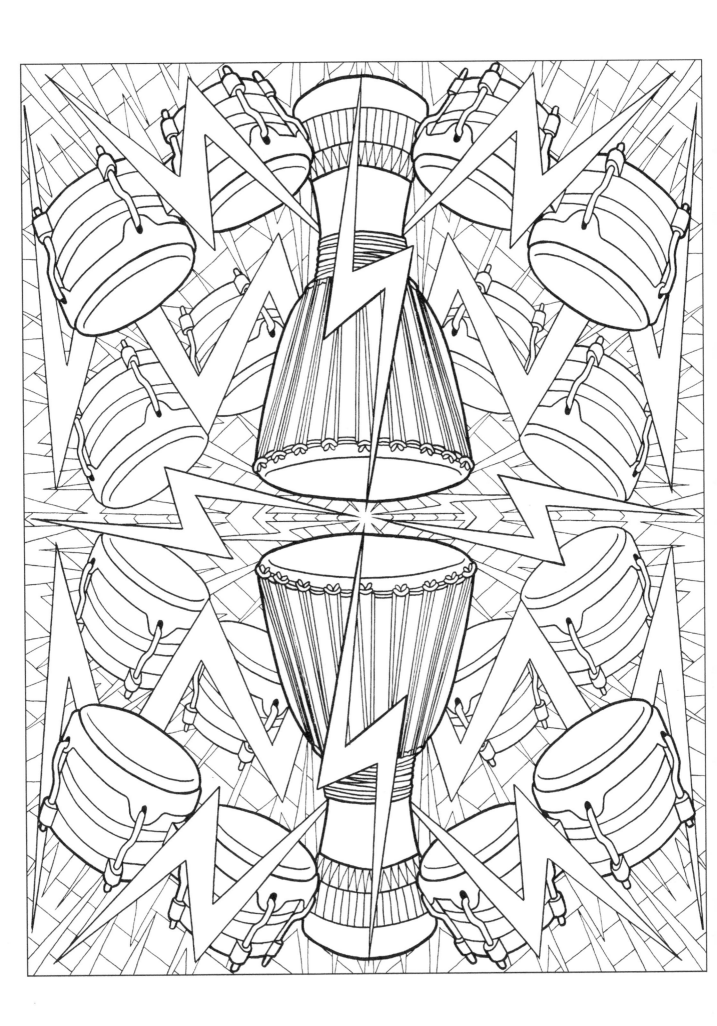

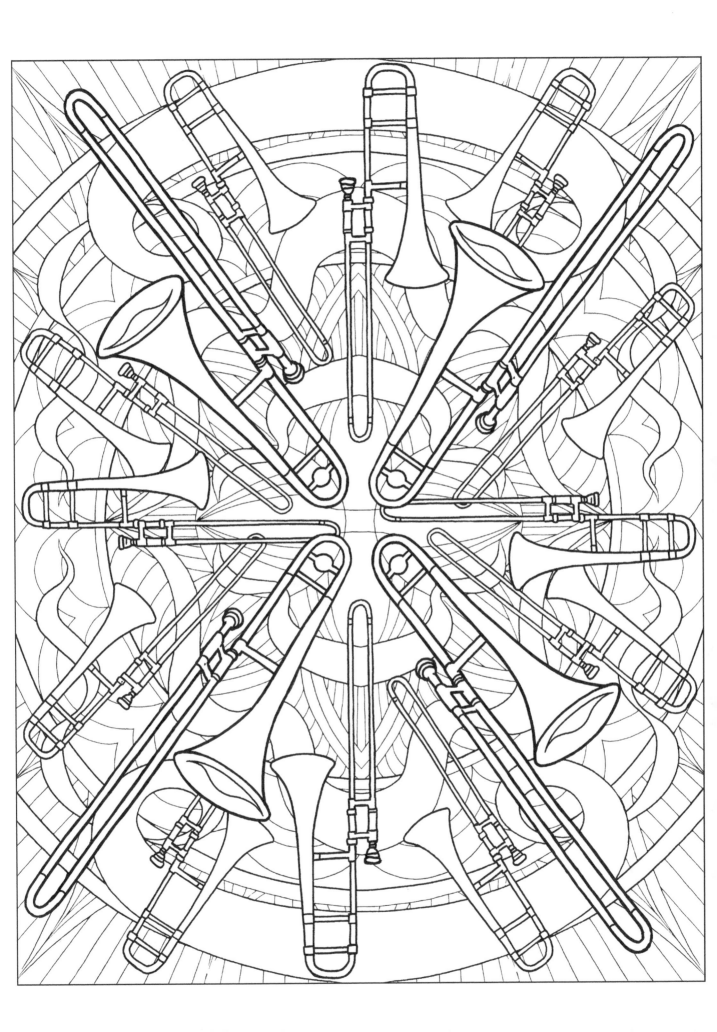

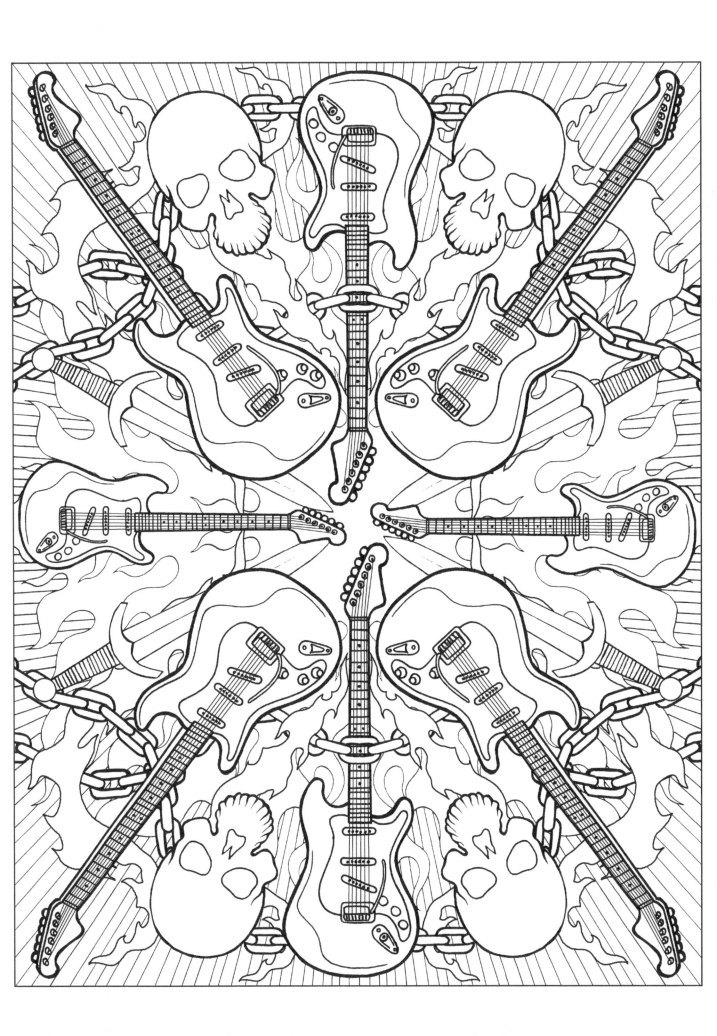

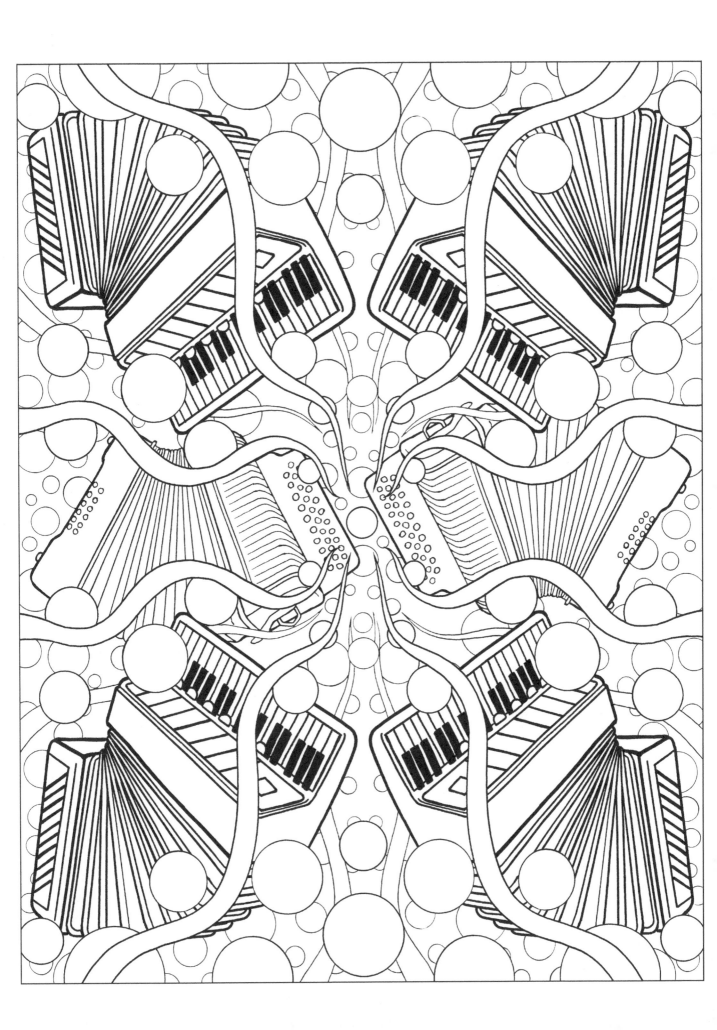

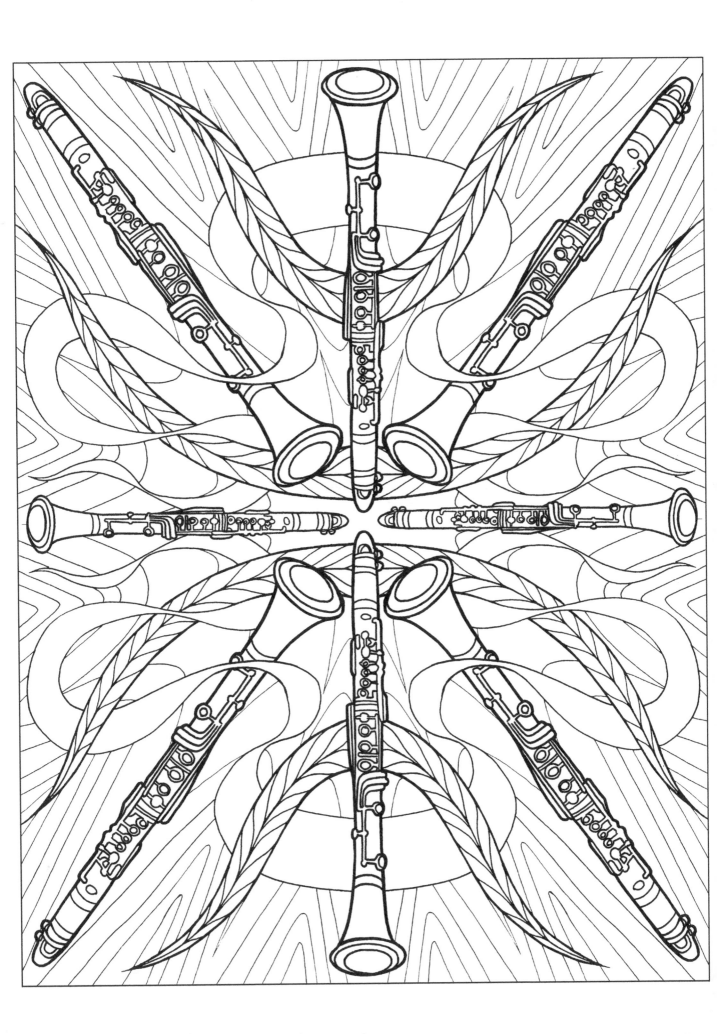

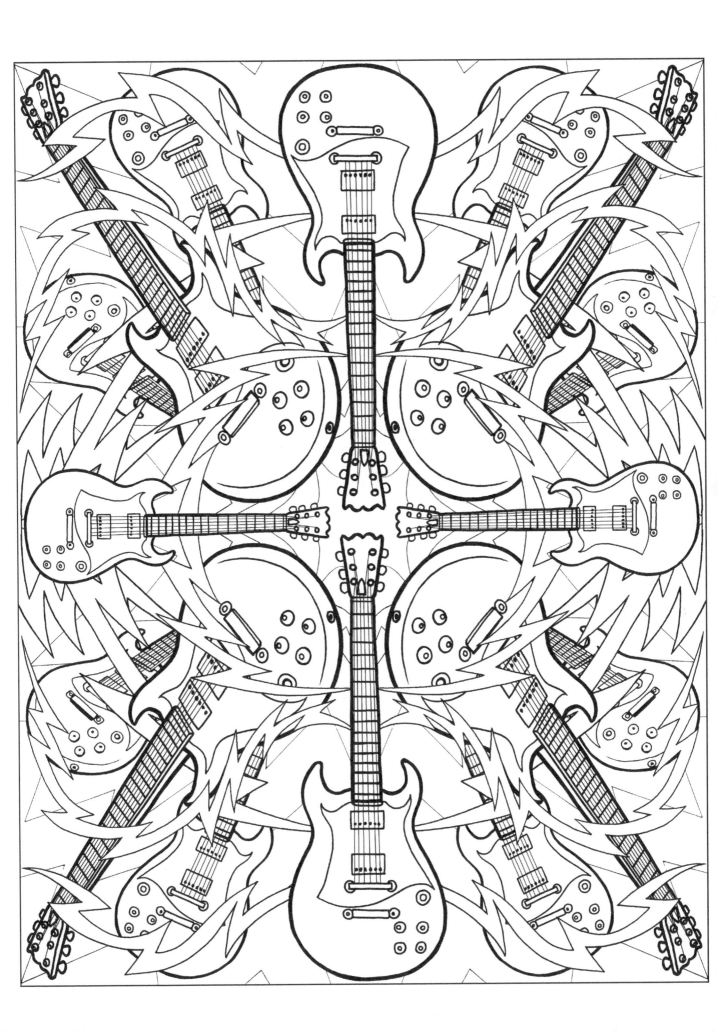

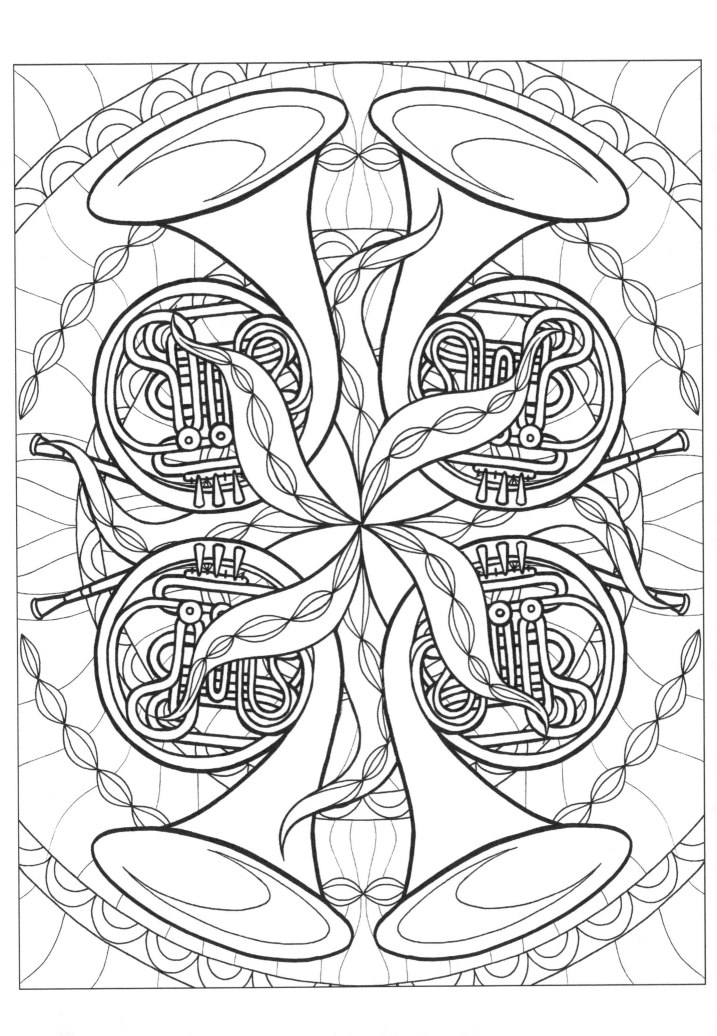

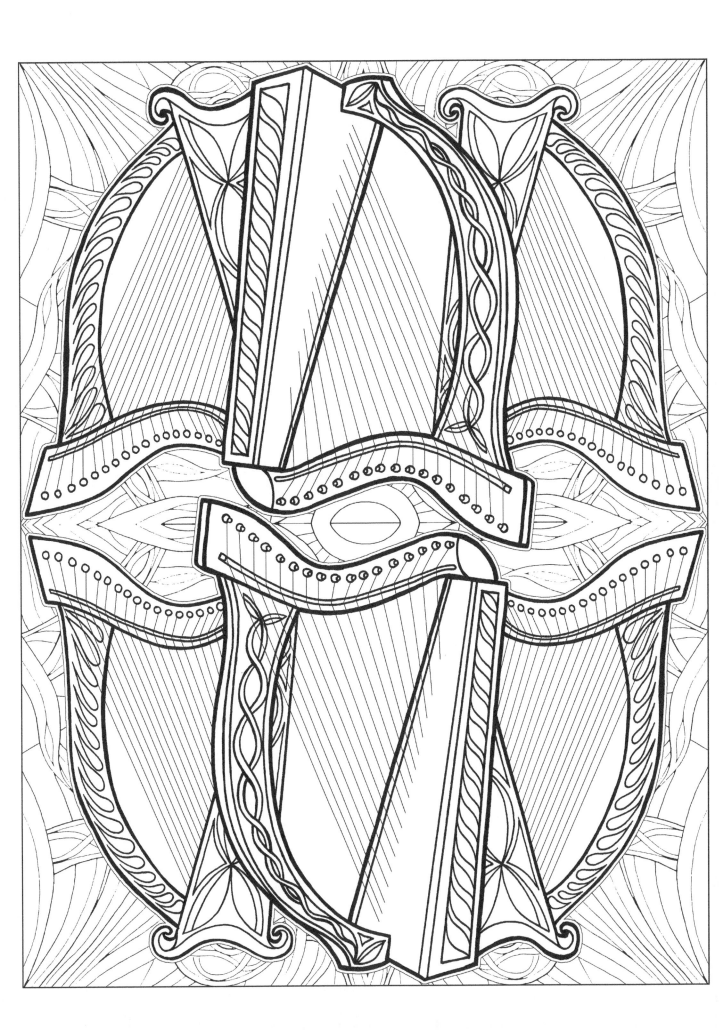

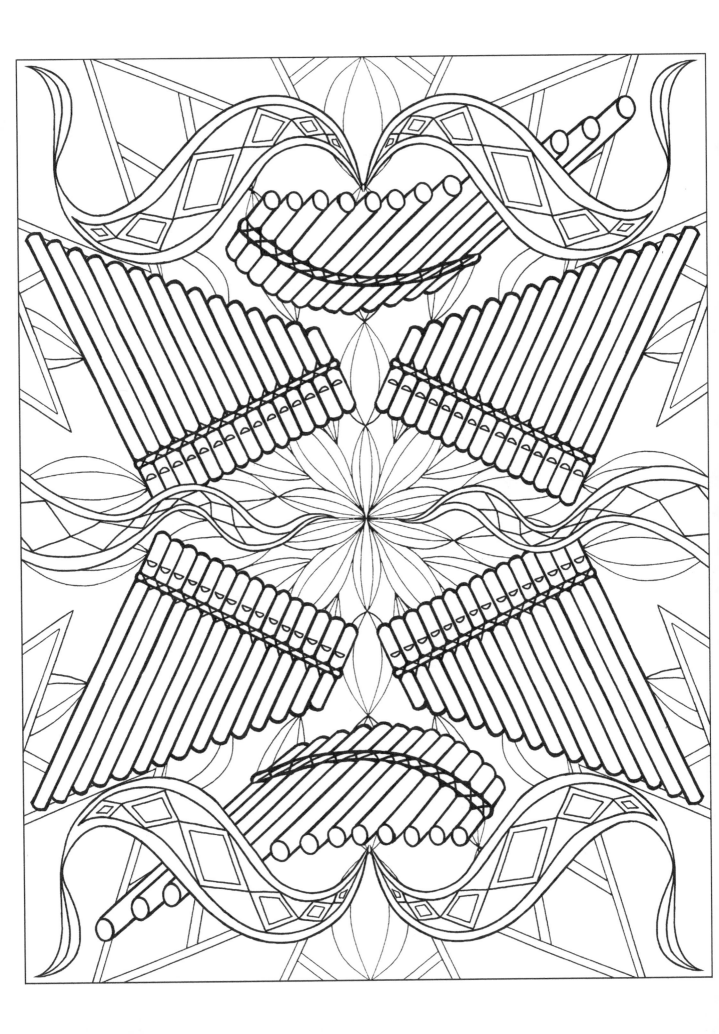

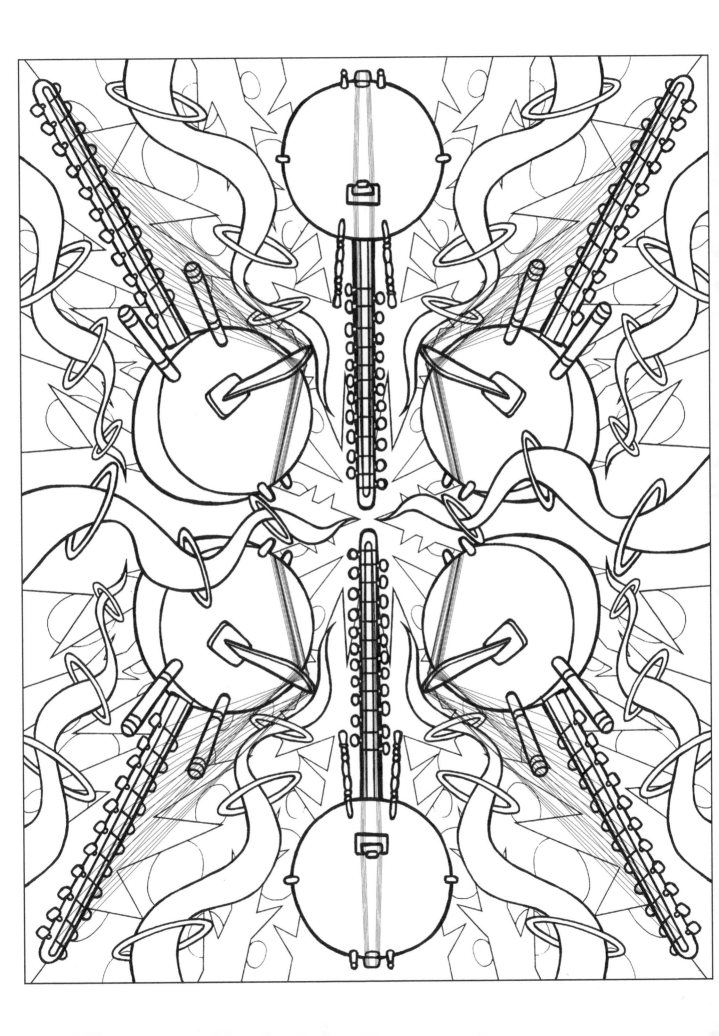